LAURIE BERKNER
SONGBOOK

UPDATED EDITION

PLAYBACK+
Speed • Pitch • Balance • Loop

To access audio, visit:
www.halleonard.com/mylibrary

Enter Code
5887-2301-8783-1753

ISBN 979-835012426-2

HAL•LEONARD®
A Muse Group Company

Visit Hal Leonard Online at
www.halleonard.com

World headquarters, contact:
Hal Leonard
7777 West Bluemound Road
Milwaukee, WI 53213
Email: info@halleonard.com

In Europe, contact:
Hal Leonard Europe Limited
Dettingen Way
Bury St Edmunds, Suffolk, IP33 3YB
Email: info@halleonardeurope.com

In Australia, contact:
Hal Leonard Australia Pty. Ltd.
4 Lentara Court
Cheltenham, Victoria, 3192 Australia
Email: info@halleonard.com.au

ABCD MEDLEY

Arrangement by Laurie Berkner

Strumming pattern:
Happy Swing feel
C F C G C G C
A B C D E F G, H I J K L M N O P,
Twin - kle, twin - kle, lit - tle star, how I won - der what you are.
G C G C G C G
Q R S, T U V, Dou - ble - U X, Y and Z.
Up a - bove the world so high, like a dia - mond in the sky.
C C7 F C G C G
Now I know my A - B - Cs. Next time, won't you sing with
Twin - kle, twin - kle, lit - tle star, how I won - der what you
C
me? are. Ba - da - da dup, ba. Ba - da - da dup, ba. Ba - da - da dup, ba. Ba - da - da
C
dup, ba. Row, row, row your boat gen - tly down the stream. Mer - ri - ly, mer - ri - ly, mer - ri - ly, mer - ri - ly,
G C D
life is but a dream. Row, row, row your boat gen - tly down the stream. Mer - ri - ly, mer - ri - ly, mer - ri - ly, mer - ri - ly,
1 A D 2 A A7 D Dsus D
life is but a dream. life is but a dream. Ba - da - da
C
dup, ba. Ba - da - da dup, ba. Ba - da - da dup, ba.

C G C G C
Frè - re Jac - ques, Frè - re Jac - ques, dor - mez - vous, dor - mez - vous?
Are you sleep - ing, are you sleep - ing, Broth - er John, Broth - er John?
(straight eighths)
G C G C
Son - nez les ma - ti - nes, son - nez les ma - ti - nes. Ding dang dong. Ding dang dong.
Morn - ing bells are ring - ing, morn - ing bells are ring - ing. Ding dang dong. Ding dang dong.
G C G C
(swing eighths)
Ding dang dong. Ding dang dong. Ba - da - da dup, ba. Ba - da - da dup, ba. Ba - da - da
C C7 F C
dup, ba. Ba - da - da - dup, ba. Oh, A B C D E F G,
G C G C G C G
H I J K L M N O P, Q R S, T U V,
C G C G C C7 F C
Dou - ble - U X, Y and Z. Now I know my A - B - Cs.
G C G G7 C F C
Next time, won't you sing with me?

THE AIRPLANE SONG

Words and Music by Laurie Berkner

Strumming pattern:
Happy Swing feel
A D E A D
1. Get in your air - planes and off we go. Go - in' to the park is first, you know.
2.–4. See additional lyrics
E A A7 D
Now slow it down and land on the ground. And
E
when you get out, you're gon - na jump all a - round.
To Coda
1, 2
A D E A
D E A A7 D Dm A E A
3
Fast Waltz
A
Get round.
D E A D E A
A7 D Dm A E
Tempo I
A
D.C. al Coda
Get
CODA
A D E A D E A A7 D Dm A
round.
(Vocal 1st time only)

1 E
2 E
A D E
5. Get back in your air - planes, it's time to go home. Your
A D E A A7
fam - i - ly and friends are wait - ing, you know. Now slow it down and
Slightly slower
D E A D A
land on the ground. And come sit down in your own home - town.

Additional Lyrics

2. Get back in your airplanes and off we go.
Goin' to California is next, you know.
Now slow it down and land on the ground.
And when you get out, you're gonna spin all around.

3. Get back in your airplanes and off we go.
Goin' to New York City is next, you know.
Now slow it down and land on the ground.
And when you get out, you're gonna gallop all around.

4. Get back in your airplanes and off we go.
Goin' to the playground is next, you know.
Now slow it down and land on the ground.
And when you get out, you're gonna dance all around.

ALL THE PLANETS

Words and Music by Laurie Berkner

Strumming pattern:
Moderately fast
Am F C G
All the plan - ets spin-ning 'round, each of them is love - ly.
All the plan - ets up in space, I wish I could see them.
What if they were on the ground in-stead of up a - bove me?
In my rock - et - ship we'd race, or I'd pre - tend to be them. What-
I would say hel - lo and tell them what I know.
ev - er game we'd play, this is what I'd say.
C Em
Mer - cu - ry's the mes - sen - ger and Ve - nus is the eve - ning star.
F G
Plan - et Earth, she is our moth - er. Mars is red and he's her broth - er.
C Em
Ju - pi - ter is king, Sat - urn wears the rings.
F G
U - ra - nus is mo - tion and Nep - tune is the o - cean.
Oh, na na na na na, na na na na na,
na na na na na na na, na na na na na na.

C Em
Na na na na na, na na na na na,
F G
na na na na na na na na, na na na na na.
Am F C G Am
F C G Am
All the plan - ets
F C G C
rit.
spin - ning 'round, and each of them is love - ly.

BOOTS

Words and Music by Laurie Berkner

Strumming pattern (intro and outro):

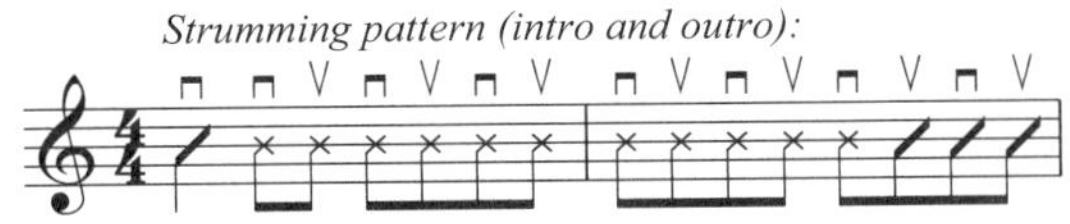

Strumming pattern (verse):

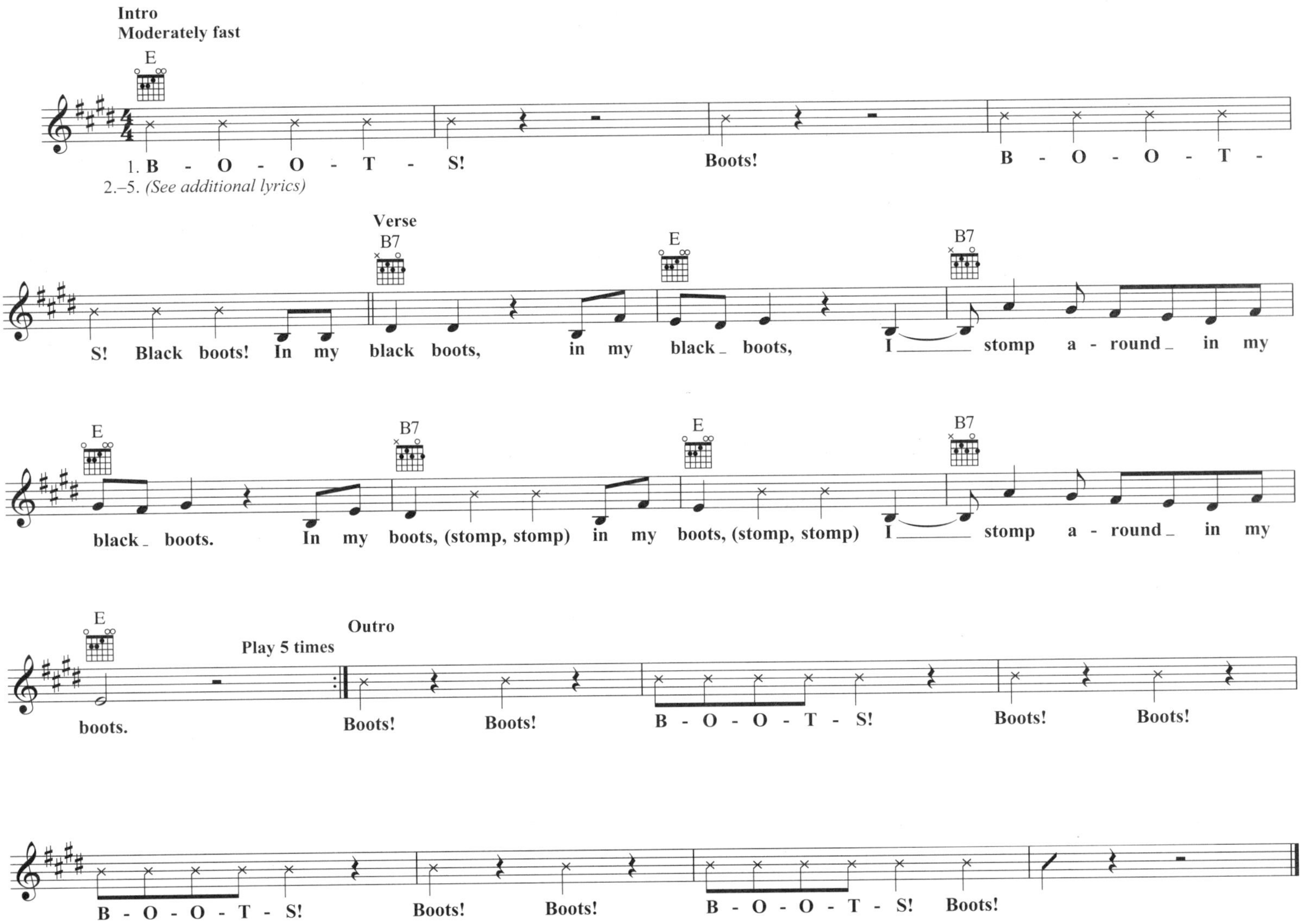
Intro
Moderately fast
E
1. B - O - O - T - S! Boots! B - O - O - T -
2.–5. (See additional lyrics)
Verse
B7
E
B7
S! Black boots! In my black boots, in my black_ boots, I_____ stomp a - round_ in my
E
B7
E
B7
black_ boots. In my boots, (stomp, stomp) in my boots, (stomp, stomp) I_____ stomp a - round_ in my
E
Play 5 times
Outro
boots. Boots! Boots! B - O - O - T - S! Boots! Boots!
B - O - O - T - S! Boots! Boots! B - O - O - T - S! Boots!

Additional Lyrics

2. B-O-O-T-S! Boots!
B-O-O-T-S! Brown boots!
In my brown boots, in my brown boots,
I stomp around in my brown boots.
In my boots, (stomp, stomp) in my boots, (stomp, stomp)
I stomp around in my boots.

3. B-O-O-T-S! Boots!
B-O-O-T-S! Frog boots!
In my frog boots, in my frog boots,
I jump around in my frog boots.
In my boots, (ribbit, ribbit) in my boots, (ribbit, ribbit)
I jump around in my boots.

4. B-O-O-T-S! Boots!
B-O-O-T-S! Dancing boots!
In my dancing boots, in my dancing boots,
I dance around in my dancing boots.
In my boots, (ooh, ooh) in my boots, (ooh, ooh)
I dance around in my boots.

5. B-O-O-T-S! Boots!
B-O-O-T-S! Rain boots!
In my rain boots, in my rain boots,
I splash around in my rain boots.
In my boots, (splish, splash) in my boots, (splish, splash)
I splash around in my boots.

DOWN DOWN BABY

Arrangement by Laurie Berkner

Moderately fast
N.C.
Down, down, ba - by, down by the roll - er coast - er. Sweet, sweet ba - by, I'll
never let you go. Shim - my, shim - my, co - coa pop. Shim - my, shim - my, pow!
Shim - my, shim - my, co - coa pop. Shim - my, shim - my, pow! Grand - ma, Grand - ma,
sick in bed. She called the doc - tor and the doc - tor said: Let's
get the rhy - thm of the head. Ding dong. Let's get the rhy - thm of the
head. Ding dong. Let's get the rhy - thm of the hands. (clap clap) Let's
get the rhy - thm of the hands. (clap clap) Let's get the rhy - thm of the
feet. Stomp stomp. Let's get the rhy - thm of the feet. Stomp stomp. Let's
get the rhy - thm of the Hot Dog. Let's get the rhy - thm of the
Hot Dog. Put it all to - geth - er and what have you got? Ding
dong, (clap clap) stomp stomp, Hot Dog!

BUBBLES

Words and Music by Laurie Berkner

Strumming pattern:
Fast, driving Rock
Guitar: Am
(Capo II)
Piano: Bm
F
G
The wa-ter's start - ed run - ning, the tub is fill - ing up.
My boat is com - ing through, (Toot, toot!) and here comes duck - y, too. (Quack,
C
D
G
A
I can't wait to get in - side. I've got my duck and my boat and my pour - ing cup.
quack!) They like to splash, they like to hide and take each oth - er for a ride.
Am
Bm
F
G
I stick my toe in. Now there's no go - ing back.
I'll wash my bod - y. I'll do my front, you do my back.
C
D
G
A
The wa - ter's call - ing me. It says: Go get those
Check out my beard and my mous - tache made out of
C
D
G
A
bub - bles in the bath, bub - bles in the bath, bub - bles in the bath - tub. Pop, pop, pop, pop,
F
G
C
D
G
A
pop. I'll try to pop, pop, pop them all, those
C
D
G
A
bub - bles in the bath, bub - bles in the bath, bub - bles in the bath - tub. Pop, pop, pop, pop,
F
G
C
D
F
G
pop. Pour out a wa - ter - fall. I can

make a wa - ter - fall.
make a wa - ter - fall,
a wa - ter - fall,
a wa - ter...
Bub - bles in the bath, bub - bles in the bath, bub - bles in the bath - tub.
Pop, pop, pop, pop, pop.
Pop, pop, pop, pop, pop.
Pop, pop, pop, pop, pop.
Pop, pop, pop, pop,
Play 3 times
pop.

CANDY CANE JANE

Words and Music by Laurie Berkner

Strumming pattern (verse):
Strumming pattern (chorus):
Moderately
Verse
Guitar: (Capo I)
Piano:
E A/B E A/B E
F B♭/C F B♭/C F
Her name was Can-dy Cane Jane. Her horse had a can-dy cane mane. She sat by the
Can-dy Cane Jane. She lived on Can-dy Cane Lane. And it was
B E/B B E B A B
C F/C C F C B♭ C
win-dow - pane and watched the snow come down. His name was
per-fect-ly plain that she liked to have fun. To - geth - er,
E A/B E A/B E
F B♭/C F B♭/C F
Gum - drop Joe. He liked to play in that snow. And so to -
Jane and Joe, they made a man out of snow. And all the
D.S. (Instrumental)
B E/B B E B A B
C F/C C F C B♭ C
geth - er they'd go for a ride on the horse with the mane made of can-dy canes.
snow-balls they'd throw filled the lane where they rode on the horse with the can-dy-cane mane.
(Instrumental ends)
Chorus
D A B D
E♭ B♭ C E♭
Gid - dy - up, gid - dy - up, gid - dy - up, go! Gid - dy - up,
To Coda
A B D C♯m
B♭ C E♭ Dm
gid - dy - up, gid - dy - up, oh! Let's go gal - lop - ing, gal - lop - ing,

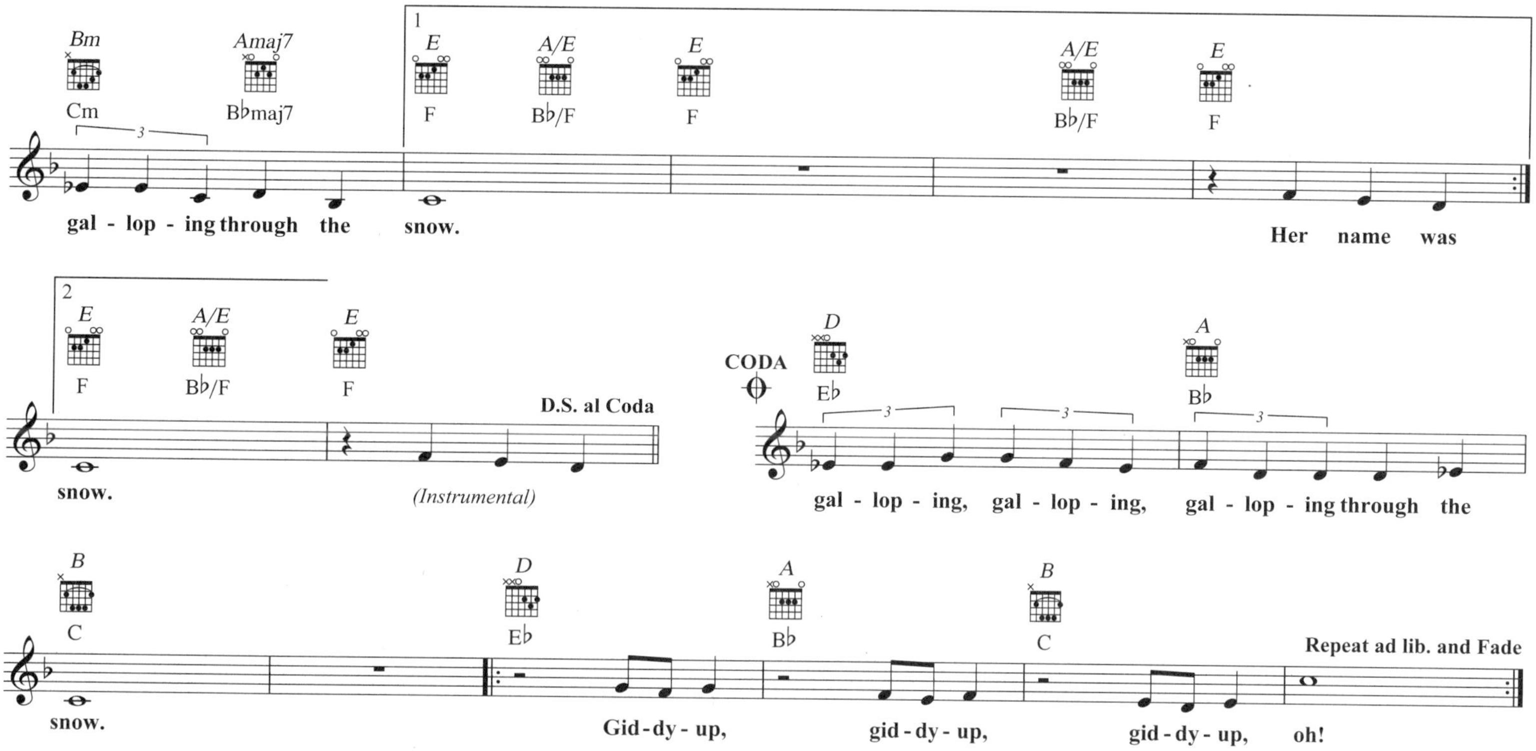
Bm Amaj7 E A/E E A/E E
Cm B♭maj7 F B♭/F F B♭/F F
gal - lop - ing through the snow.
Her name was
E A/E E
F B♭/F F
D.S. al Coda
snow.
(Instrumental)
CODA
D A
E♭ B♭
gal - lop - ing, gal - lop - ing, gal - lop - ing through the
B D A B
C E♭ B♭ C
Repeat ad lib. and Fade
snow.
Gid - dy - up, gid - dy - up, gid - dy - up, oh!

FAST AND SLOW
(THE RABBIT AND THE TURTLE)

Words and Music by Laurie Berkner

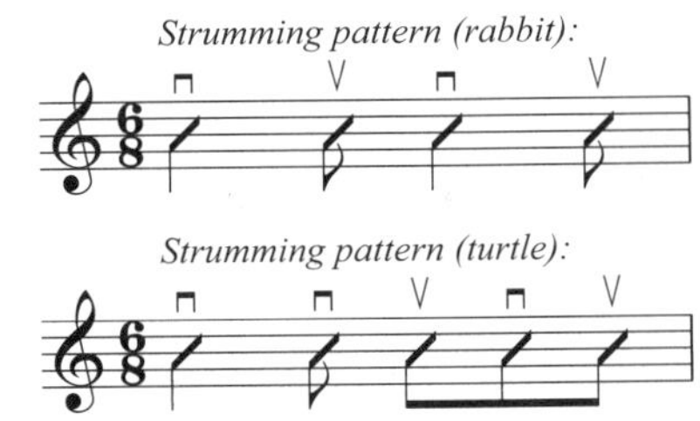
Strumming pattern (rabbit):
Strumming pattern (turtle):

Quickly
RABBIT:
D A D A D G D G D A D G
I don't wan-na go slow, I go fast. I'm a rab-bit, I hop and I jump and I dash. And I'll go whiz-zing by in the blink of an eye, like a jet en-gine air-plane that speeds through the sky. I don't
Instrumental
1, 3
wan-na go slow, I go fast. (Instrumental)
2, 4
Instrumental ends
TURTLE:
A D A D G D G D A D G D A
I don't wan-na go fast, I go slow. That's the way that I move; I'm a tur-tle, you know.
You don't wan-na go slow, you go fast. And you may find you're miss-ing the world you go past.
Join me as I crawl by. We can laugh, we can cry, we can breathe, we can sigh, we can talk a-bout why we don't wan-na go fast, we go
Crick-ets sing-ing their sound, gold-en leaves on the ground. You might find some-thing new that you would-n't have found if you nev-er went slow, on-ly
To Coda

D
D.S. al Coda
(with repeat)
RABBIT:
slow.
I don't
CODA
D
fast.
So, won't you slow down and wait for
me? Take it slow, take it slow, take it slow.
G
A
D
Come on, slow down. We can
share all the new things we see when we're slow. Here we go. To-
G
A
D
geth-er we're slow.
RABBIT:
And oth-er times, we can go fast!
A
D

FIREFLIES

Words and Music by Laurie Berkner

Gently
N.C.
Ha - oom, ha - oom, ha - oom, ha - oom,
Fire - flies dance and fire - flies glow in the night, in the night, in the night.
'Round and 'round with - out a sound, mak - ing a lan - tern of light.
Fe - lix lands on my left hand and Fri - da lands on my right.
Each one flash - es si - lent - ly like ti - ny lit - tle stars beam - ing bright.
First he blinks and then she winks, and they fly through the sky, out of sight.
Fire - flies dance and fire - flies glow in the night, in the night, in the night. Ha -
oom, ha - oom, ha - oom, ha - oom. oom. In the
night, in the night, in the night, in the night. Good - night, in the night, in the night.
rit.

FIVE DAYS OLD

Words and Music by Laurie Berkner

Strumming pattern:

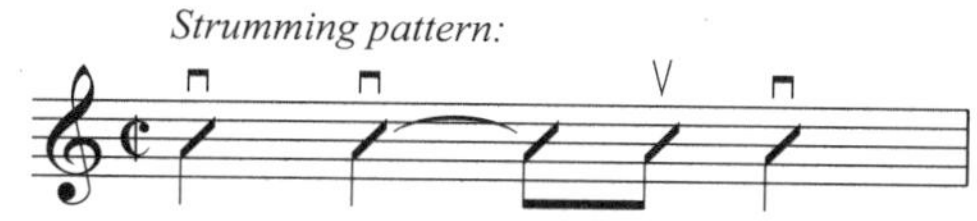

Additional Lyrics

2., 6. And I'm jumpin' up, I'm one day old,
And I'm jumpin' up, I'm two days old.
I'm jumpin' up, I'm three days old,
And I'm jumpin' up, I'm four days old.
One day, I'll be a year.
Then I'll be two, then three, then four.
But as for now, I'm jumpin' up.
I'm five days old and no days more.

3. I'm clappin' my hands, I'm one day old,
I'm clappin' my hands, I'm two days old.
Clappin' my hands, I'm three days old,
I'm clappin' my hands, I'm four days old.
One day, I'll be a year.
Then I'll be two, then three, then four.
But as for now, I'm clappin' my hands.
I'm five days old and no days more.

4. And I'm kickin' out my legs, I'm one day old,
I'm kickin' out my legs, I'm two days old.
I'm kickin' out my legs, I'm three days old,
I'm kickin' out my legs, I'm four days old.
One day, I'll be a year.
Then I'll be two, then three, then four.
But as for now, I'm kickin' out my legs.
I'm five days old and no days more.

(slower)

5. And I'm gettin' tired, I'm one day old,
I'm gettin' tired, I'm two days old.
I'm gettin' tired, I'm three days old,
And I'm gettin' tired, I'm four days old.
One day, I'll be a year.
Then I'll be two, then three, then four.
But as for now, I'm gettin' pretty tired.
And I'm five days old and no days more.

FRUIT SALAD SALSA

Words and Music by Laurie Berkner

Picking pattern (verse):
Strumming pattern (chorus):
Verse
Moderately, in 2
F
C7
Here come the man - goes with one hand out. And
Here come the pine - ap - ples, shake, shake, shake.
here come the ap - ples with one hand out. And
Here come the or - an - ges, shake, shake, shake.
here come pa - pa - yas with one hand out,
Here come ba - nan - as, go shake, shake, shake,
all for the fruit sal - ad sal - sa.
all for the fruit sal - ad sal - sa.
1
2
Chorus
And then they jump, jump, jump, jump, jump, jump in - to the bowl.
They jump, jump, jump, jump, jump, jump in - to the bowl.
And then they jump, jump, jump, jump, jump, jump in - to the bowl,
all for the fruit sal - ad sal - sa.
Verse
Then all the

C7
fruits, they go spin - ning a - round, spin - ning and tum - bling and
F
C7
mix - ing a - round. Then all the fruits, they go spin - ning a -
F
round, all for the fruit sal - ad sal - sa. And ev - 'ry - bod - y goes
Chorus
F
C7
in and shake, shake, shake. And ev - 'ry - bod - y goes
Instrumental
F
out and shake, shake, shake. And ev - 'ry - bod - y goes
C7
in and shake, shake, shake, oh,
F
Verse
F
all for the fruit sal - ad sal - sa. I hear the
C7
man - goes say, "Let's eat." I hear the ap - ples say,
F
C7
"It's time to eat." I hear pa - pa - yas say, "Let's
F
eat." All for the fruit sal - ad sal - sa.

THE GOLDFISH

Words and Music by Laurie Berkner

Strumming pattern (chorus and bridge):
Strumming pattern (verse):
Moderately, freely
C G C
Lots of lit - tle fish were sleep-ing on a rock in the bot - tom of ___ the o - cean. They
Bright half-time feel
G
lift - ed up their heads and they shook out their tails, ___ and they said, ___ "Let's go
Chorus
C C G
swim-ming. Let's go swim-ming, let's ___ go swim-ming. Yeah, let's go
C G
swim-ming. Let's ___ go swim-ming, let's ___ go swim-ming in the bot - tom of ___ the
Verse
C C
o - cean." Then the lit - tle fish got so ver - y ver - y ti - red that they
G C
came back to the rock. And they put down their heads and they put down their tails ___ and they
Bridge
G C N.C.
took a lit - tle nap. 1. And when they woke up,
2., 3. (See additional lyrics)
(Spoken:) they were feeling a little bit dirty.
So they took a shower.
Bright half-time feel
C
And they washed their hair and they washed their ears. ___

G
And they washed their tum - mies and they washed their beards.
C C7 F
And they washed their nose and they washed their toes.
C G N.C. G C
And then they said: (Spoken:) Wait a minute! We're fish!
N.C.
(Spoken:) We don't take showers! 1, 2 Let's go 3 Let's go swim - ming, let's go
G C
swim-ming. Yeah, let's go swim-ming. Let's go swim-ming, let's go
G 1 C 2 C
swim-ming in the bot - tom of the o - cean." Let's go o - cean."

Additional Lyrics

2. And when they woke up,
(Spoken:) they decided to brush their teeth.
(Sung:) So they got out their toothbrush and their toothpaste.
And they squeezed a little on, they tried not to waste.
And they put it in their mouth, they brushed north and south.
Ch-ch-ch-ch-ch-ch-ch.
Ch-ch-ch-ch-ch-ch-ch.
And then they said:
(Spoken:) Wait a minute! We're fish! We don't brush our teeth!
(Sung:) Let's go... *(To Chorus)*

3. And when they woke up,
(Spoken:) they decided to ride their bicycles.
(Sung:) So they rode to the left and they rode to the right.
And they rode all day and they rode all night.
They rode down the hill, and then faster still.
And then they said:
(Spoken:) Wait a minute! We're fish! We don't ride bicycles!

GOODNIGHT

Words and Music by Laurie Berkner

Strumming pattern:
Moderately
D A A7 G N.C.
1. I'm a lit-tle frog and my dad-dy loves me. I'm a lit-tle frog and my mom-my loves me. And
2.–4. (See additional lyrics)
when they tuck me in to say good-night, they say, "Rib-bit, rib-bit, rib-bit, good-night." Good-night,
good-night. Good-night, lit-tle frog, good-night. Good-night,
1–3
good-night. "Rib-bit, rib-bit, rib-bit, good-night."
4
Good-night, good-night, good-night. Good-night, good-night.
Good-night, ev-'ry-bod-y, sleep tight, lit-tle dar-lin', good-night. Good-night, good-night.
1, 2
3
Good-night, good-night, good-night. Good-night,

Additional Lyrics

2. I'm a little owl... *(Hoo, hoo, hoo.)*
3. I'm a little tiger... *(Rrahh, rrahh.)*
4. I'm a little kid... *(Goodnight, honey.)*

I'M A MESS

Words and Music by Laurie Berkner

Brightly
N.C.
I'm a mess. I'm a mess. I'm a big old mess - y mess. From the
north to the south and the east to the west, what I am is a real - ly, real - ly,
To Coda
real - ly big mess! 1. I try to get dressed, but I make a mess. I jump in the pud- dles, and
2. (See additional lyrics)
can you guess? I make mud pies when the mud is fresh, and then, uh - oh, I
1
made a big mess! I'm a
2
made a big mess! I'm a
D.S. al Coda
CODA
real - ly big mess!

Additional Lyrics

2. Now, eating messy food, you know it's the best.
'Cause no matter what I do, I make a big mess.
Get dinner on my jacket, breakfast on my vest,
Lunch in my socks, uh-oh, what a mess!

I KNOW A CHICKEN

Words and Music by Laurie Berkner

Strumming pattern (chorus):
Strumming pattern (verse):
Chorus
Moderate, bluesy Swing
E7
Oh, I know a chick-en (I know a chick-en) and she laid an egg (and she laid an egg).
A7
Oh, I know a chick-en (I know a chick-en) and she
E7
laid an egg (and she laid an egg).
B7
Oh, my good-ness.
To Coda
E7
(Oh, my good-ness.) It's a shak-y egg. (It's a shak-y egg.)
(Spoken:) Now, shake your eggs.
N.C.
Verse
Quickly, in 2
E7
1. Shake 'em fast.
2., 3. (See additional lyrics)
Shake 'em fast.
Shake 'em
A7
fast.
E7
Shake 'em fast.

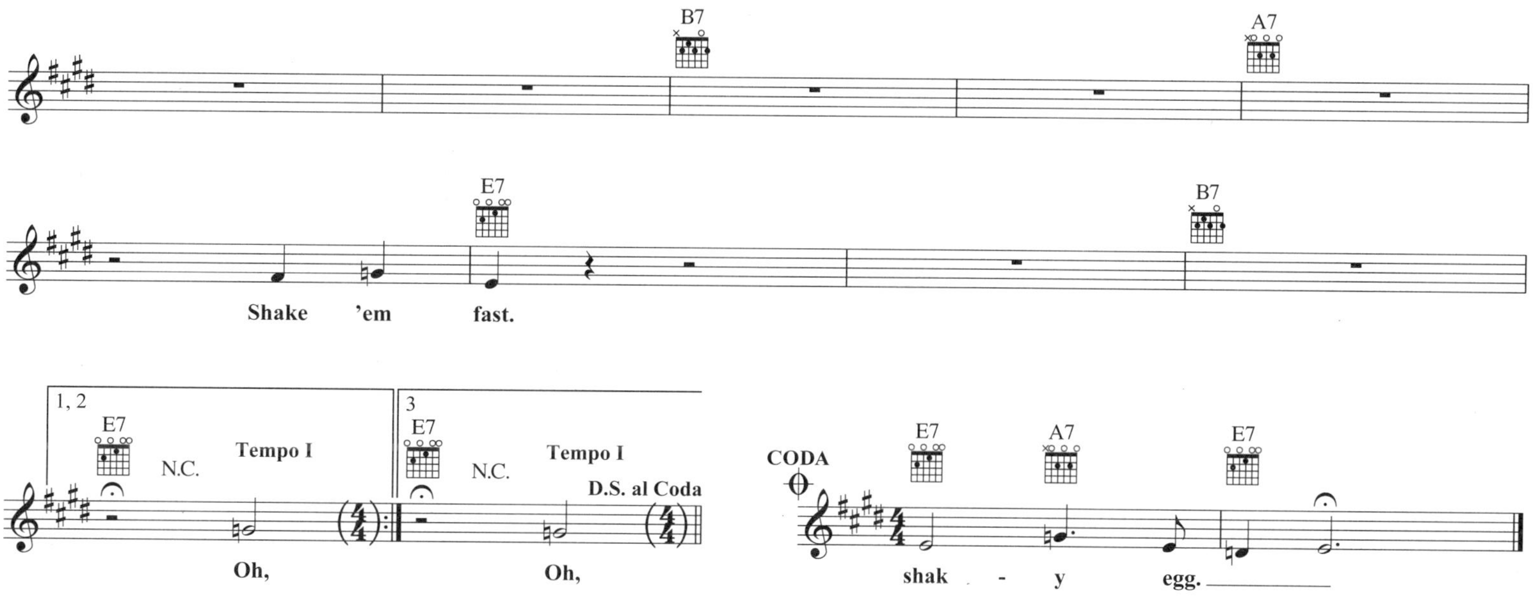

Additional Lyrics

(slow blues)
2. Now, shake 'em slow.
You know how it goes.
Shake 'em slow.
You know how it goes.
Shake 'em fast. (quickly, in 2)
Oh, shake those eggs.

(6/8 feel)
3. Can you shake 'em in a circle?
Oh, 'round and 'round.
Don't you let 'em touch the ground.
'Cause you shake 'em 'round and 'round.
Now, shake 'em up and down. (ska beat)
Oh, shake 'em up and down.
Shake those eggs.

A LULLABY

Words and Music by Laurie Berkner

Strumming pattern:
Gently
E B A
A lull - a - by is not good - bye. It on - ly means I'll
B E
see you in the morn - ing. A lull - a - by is a
B A B
way that I can sing you to sleep while you're yawn - ing.
A F#m B
So let me rock you and
E C#m 4fr F#
you can dream. I can't
A B
wait to see you a - gain.
Bsus B E B
'Cause a lull - a - by is not good - bye.

A B
It's some - thing warm _ that I can give _ to you. And a
E B A
lull - a - by _ is a song that I _ sing be - cause _ I
B A
love you, yes, _ I _ do. So lay your
F♯m B E C♯m
head down and rest.
F♯ A
I can't wait to see _ you _ a - gain _
B Bsus B E
and sing you an - oth - er lull - a - by.
B A
B E B
A lull - a - by _ is not good - bye. _
A B
rit.
It on - ly means _ I'll see you in _ the morn - ing. _

MONSTER BOOGIE

Words and Music by Laurie Berkner

Strumming pattern (verse):
Strumming pattern (chorus):
March beat
Verse
D
A
A7
G
I'm the big - gest mon - ster that you've ev - er seen. My eyes are pur - ple and my teeth are green. I'm big and I'm scar - y. You know what I mean. This is what I like to do. I do the
big - gest mon - ster that you've ev - er seen. My eyes are yel - low and my teeth are green. I'm big and I'm hair - y. You know what I mean This is what I like to do. I do the
Chorus
Bm
mon - ster boog - ie, the mon - ster boog - ie, the mon - ster boog - ie 'round the room. Ev - 'ry - bod - y does the mon - ster boog - ie, the mon - ster boog - ie, the mon - ster boog - ie. So can you. I'm the
mon - ster wig - gle, the mon - ster wig - gle, the mon - ster wig - gle 'round the room. Ev - 'ry - bod - y does the mon - ster wig - gle, the mon - ster wig - gle, the mon - ster wig - gle. So can you.
1
2
3
(Spoken:) Rraaaahhh!

OPEN SHUT THEM

Arrangement by Laurie Berkner

Steadily
N.C.
O - pen, shut them. O - pen, shut them. Give a lit - tle clap, clap, clap.
O - pen, shut them. O - pen, shut them. Put them in your lap, lap, lap.
To Coda
Creep them, crawl, them. Creep them, crawl them, right up to your chin, chin, chin.
rit.
Fast
O - pen wide your lit - tle mouth ahh, but do not let them in.
Tempo I
Loud and qui - et, loud and qui - et. Loud - er, loud - er, shhh, qui - et.
D.C. al Coda
Loud and qui - et, loud and qui - et. Loud! Shhh, qui - et.
CODA
nose, nose nose. Creep them, crawl, them. Creep them, crawl them, right down to your
toes, toes, toes. Shake them, shake them. Roll them, roll them. Make them in - to lit - tle fists.
rit.
Fast
Shake them, shake them. Roll, roll, roll. Then you blow a kiss, kiss, kiss. Mwah!

MY FAMILY

Words and Music by Laurie Berkner

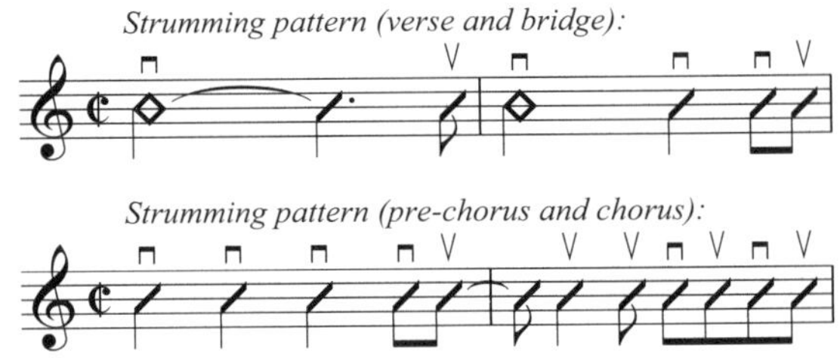
Strumming pattern (verse and bridge):
Strumming pattern (pre-chorus and chorus):

Intro
Moderately, in 2
Guitar: (Capo I)
Piano:
A D A D G D A D A E
B♭ E♭ B♭ E♭ A♭ E♭ B♭ E♭ B♭ F
F - A - M - I - L - Y, F - A - M - I - L - Y, F - A - M - I - L - Y, fam - i - ly.
Verse
A E G D A E G D
B♭ F A♭ E♭ B♭ F A♭ E♭
When you're in my heart, you're in my fam - i - ly. When I'm in your heart, I'm in your fam - i - ly. When you're in my heart, you're in my fam - i - ly. When I'm in your heart, I'm in your fam - i - ly.
Pre-Chorus
A E G D A E
B♭ F A♭ E♭ B♭ F
Fa - thers, moth - ers, sis - ters, broth - ers, cous - ins, friends, sons and daugh - ters, un - cles, aunts and grand - par - ents.

G D
A♭ E♭
I'm so glad you're my fam - i - ly. Oh,
Chorus
A E G
B♭ F A♭
I'm so glad you're my fam - i - ly. I'm so glad
D A
E♭ B♭
you're my fam - i - ly I'm so glad
E G D
F A♭ E♭
you're my fam - i - ly. I'm so glad you're my fam - i - ly.
To Coda
A
B♭
Bridge
A
B♭
And e - ven if you're far a - way, or
D A E
E♭ B♭ F
if I see you ev - er - y day, when you're in my heart to stay, you're my fam - i - ly.
D.S. al Coda
When
CODA
A
B♭
I'm so glad
E G D
F A♭ E♭
you're my fam - i - ly. I'm so glad you're my fam - i - ly.
1
Oh,
2
Outro
A D A D G D
B♭ E♭ B♭ E♭ A♭ E♭
F - A - M - I - L - Y, F - A - M - I - L - Y,
A D A E A
B♭ E♭ B♭ F B♭
F - A - M - I - L - Y, fam - i - ly. Oh, I'm so glad.

OPEN YOUR HEART

Words and Music by Laurie Berkner

Strumming pattern (verse):
Strumming pattern (pre-chorus and chorus):
Verse
Moderately bright
D N.C.
I can use my voice to sing out a song, and use my mus-cles when I'm feel - ing strong.
I can use my head to say no or yes, I can use my mouth to take in a breath.
I can use a key to o-pen a lock, I can lis-ten when the two of us talk.
A N.C.
I can use my arms for hug-ging you tight, and use my pil-low when I sleep at night.
I can turn a knob to o-pen a door, and I can dance my way a-cross the floor.
I can taste my salt-y tears when I cry, or use my bod-y when I jump up high.
But
Pre-Chorus
G D Bm A
some things I can't do. That's why I need you to
Chorus
D E G D
o - pen your heart. My heart is wait - ing for you. O - pen your heart.
G D
My heart is wait - ing.
To Coda
Bridge
A E
What's in-side when I o-pen my heart?
Turn the wheel and what do I feel?
G D
I feel love when I o-pen my heart.
Do you feel it, too?
D.C. al Coda
(no repeat)
CODA
O - pen your heart.
O - pen your heart.
O - pen your heart. My heart is wait - ing.

PIG ON HER HEAD

Words and Music by Laurie Berkner

Additional Lyrics

2. My dad has got a cow on his head.
   My dad has got a cow on his head.
   My dad has got a cow on his head.
   He keeps it there all day.

3. My mom has got a sheep on her head.
   My mom has got a sheep on her head.
   My mom has got a sheep on her head.
   She keeps it there all day.

4. My sister's got an alligator on her head.
   My sister's got an alligator on her head.
   My sister's got an alligator on her head.
   She keeps it there all day.

5. My brother's got an elephant on his head.
   My brother's got an elephant on his head.
   My brother's got an elephant on his head.
   He keeps it there all day.

6. My cousin's got his hair on his head.
   My cousin's got his hair on his head.
   My cousin's got his hair on his head.
   He keeps it there all day.

7. And my dog has got a skunk on his head.
   My dog has got a skunk on his head.
   My dog has got a skunk on his head.
   And everybody ran away.

PARTY DAY

Words and Music by Laurie Berkner

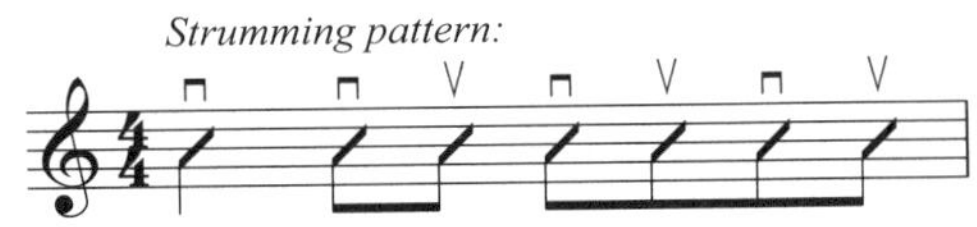
Strumming pattern:

Moderately fast
Guitar: (Capo I)
Piano:
One little ladybug called up a banana slug, a cucumber beetle and an ant. They drove to the beach, where each one of them taught that little ladybug a dance. They told stories and watched the waves, and played for hours in the sand. Then that little ladybug said to the banana slug, the beetle and the ant: Come and take my hand.
One little ladybug and a banana slug, a cucumber beetle and an ant watched as the sun went down over the little town they had built together in the sand. Cucumber beetle had a purple guitar and started to play them all a tune. That's when the ladybug turned to the banana slug, the beetle and the ant, and this is what she sang:
N.C.
I like it here with all my friends (friends, friends). I never want this day to end (end, end). 'Cause we can dance and we can play (play, play). Let's make today a party day (day, day). Let's make today a party day. Let's make today a party

D D/C# Bm Bm/A G E
E♭ E♭/D Cm Cm/B♭ A♭ F
day. 'Cause we can dance and we can play. Let's make to - day a par - ty
1 A 2 A
B♭ N.C. B♭
day. day. Oh, let's make to - day a par - ty
D D/C# Bm Bm/A
E♭ E♭/D Cm Cm/B♭
day. Let's make to - day a par - ty day. 'Cause we can dance and we can
G E A D E
A♭ F N.C. B♭ E♭ F
play. Let's make to - day a par - ty day. Oh, let's make to - day a par - ty
A D E A D E
B♭ E♭ F B♭ E♭ F
day. Mm, let's make to - day a par - ty day. Let's make to - day a par - ty
A G F G A
B♭ A♭ G♭ rit. A♭ B♭
day.

PILLOWLAND

Words and Music by Laurie Berkner

Strumming pattern:

Brightly
C F C G Am
I know a place, a king-dom far a-way, where peo-ple wear pa-ja-mas ev-'ry night and ev-'ry day, where all the hous-es, the build-ings and the trees are made of fluff-y pil-lows that are soft as they can be. We can
A feath-er o-cean and a blan-ket boat, we're rid-ing to a pil-low cas-tle through a quilt-ed moat. We'll meet the king and then we'll meet the queen. They'll show us all the pil-low se-crets no one else has seen, like how to
ride a pil-low train (Choo choo!) or drive a pil-low car, (Beep beep!) fly a mag-ic pil-low plane, (Zoom zoom!) swing on a pil-low fall-ing star. (Whee!) And when we let go, we're gon-na land in Pil-low-land. We're gon-na land in Pil-low-land.
1
2
Pil-low-land, land in

Pil - low - land. We're gon - na land in Pil - low - land.
Pil - low bread and pil - low jam on pil - low din - ner - ware. You will find me
right be - side you, throw-ing them in the air! And then we'll ask the king just one
more thing: "What do we do at night?" "We gath - er up the pil -
- lows and we have a pil - low fight!"
Land in Pil - low - land, we're gon - na land in
Pil - low - land, land in Pil - low - land. We're gon - na land in
Pil - low - land.

SHAKE YOUR BODY DOWN

Words and Music by Laurie Berkner

Strumming pattern (verse):
Strumming pattern (chorus):
Brightly
A
Do you wan-na play a game? (Yes, I wan-na play a game!) Do you wan-na play a game? (Yes, I wan-na play a game!) Well,
Verse
Bm
if you wan-na play a game, then stand up tall, tall as you can and move
D
from side to side.
A
Hold out one arm and the oth-er arm,
Bm
make your bod-y wide.
Lift your shoul-ders up,
D
roll 'em all a-round.
Chorus
A
Shake out your head, shake out your arms and shake
D G D G D A D
your bod-y down, shake it up and down. Shake, shake, shake your bod-y down.
G D A D
Clap your hands three times. One, two, three! Jump up in-to the game with me and
G D A
clap your hands three times. One, two, three! Now you can jump and I can jump (high-er, high-er).
Verse
Bm
To Coda
You can jump and I can jump (high-er, high-er). Shhh! Wave

D
your arms high. Wave your arms low. Now
A
march in place, march real - ly fast, and
Bm
march real - ly slow, march real - ly slow.
D.S. al Coda
CODA
D
Turn your-self a-round, fast as you can, till you fall to the ground.
A
N.C.
Now make a face. Fly in - to space.
(slide up the octave)
Chorus
D G D G D
Shake your head down. Shake your arms down. Shake
G D G D G D G D
your shoul-ders down. Shake your legs down. Shake your hips down. Shake your knees down and shake,
A D G D A
shake, shake your bod - y down. Clap your hands three times. One, two, three! Jump
D G D
up in - to the game with me and clap your hands three times. One, two, three! Now
A
you can jump and I can jump (high - er, high - er). You can jump and I can jump (high - er, high - er).
D A G D
You can jump and I can jump (high - er, high - er). Shake, shake, shake your bod - y down.

SUPERHERO

Words and Music by Laurie Berkner

Strumming pattern:
Brightly
D C G
1. When you're in trou - ble, I'm there on the dou - ble to help you with what - ev - er you need.
2. (See additional lyrics)
D C G
Up, up, up and a - way, I can save the day and do an - y su - per deed.
D C B♭
'Cause I have su - per pow - ers, su - per strength and su - per speed.
A N.C. Chorus G D
And I could be a su - per - he - ro. I could be a
G D C G
su - per - he - ro. And I hold my fist up high when I start to fly.
A G D
I could be a su - per - he - ro. I could be a
G D C G
su - per - he - ro. And I'm not a - fraid to stand up for what's right,
A D
an - y day or night.
1 2 N.C. (D)
I can swoop and swirl and sweep

through the sky. I can be a good friend, I can cap - ture the spies. I can de - fend your cit - y, res -
A
- cue a kit - ty. When a friend needs help, I nev - er leave them be - hind. I've got su - per sight, I've got
D
su - per stretch, and when the chase is on, there's no one I can't catch. You don't have to ask, 'cause I like
A
N.C.
to be kind. And it does - n't mat - ter who you are; ev - 'ry - bod - y shines when we are
G D G D
su - per - he - roes. Yes, we are su - per - he - roes. And we
C G A
hold our fists up high when we start to fly. You know we're
G D G D
su - per - he - roes. We can be su - per - he - roes. And we're
C G A
not a - fraid to stand up for what's right, an - y day
G D
or an - y night.

Additional Lyrics

2. Look, look, look at my comic book
And this is who you'll see:
Batman, Wonder Woman, Supergirl, Spider-Man,
Captain Marvel and me!
'Cause I am strong and I belong
To a Hero family.
And I could be a... *(To Chorus)*

TELEPHONE

Words and Music by Laurie Berkner

Brightly, in 2
N.C.
I called you on the tel - e - phone. Ring - a - ling - a - ling, you were - n't home. I
to your house, knocked on the door. Knock, knock, knock, then I knocked some more. Went
called you on the tel - e - phone. Ring - a - ling - a - ling, you were - n't home. Hel -
to your house, knocked on the door. Knock, knock, knock, then I knocked some more.
lo? (Hel - lo?) Is an - y - bod - y there? (Is an - y - bod - y there?) Hel -
lo? (Hel - lo?) No - bod - y's there. (No - bod - y's there.)
1
Went
2
So I went to sleep and dreamed of you.
Snore, shoo, snore, shoo. I went to sleep and dreamed of you.
Snore, shoo, snore, shoo. Hel - lo? (Hel - lo?) Is
an - y - bod - y there? (Is an - y - bod - y there?) Hel - lo? (Hel - lo?)

rit.
No - bod - y's there. (No - bod - y's there.) (snoring) So I
a tempo
called you on the
tel - e - phone. Ring - a - ling - a - ling, you were - n't home. I called you on the
tel - e - phone. Ring - a - ling - a - ling, you were - n't home. Ring one time.
Brring! Ring two times. Brring! Brring! Three times.
Brring! Brring! Brring! Ring four times. Brring! Brring! Brring! Brring!
(Spoken:) Hello?
(random chatting)

THESE ARE MY GLASSES

Words and Music by Laurie Berkner

Moderately
N.C.
These are my glass - es, this is my book. I put on my glass - es and o - pen up the book. Now I
read, read, read and I look, look, look. I put down my glass - es and (whoop) close up the book.
Play 3 times

WE ARE THE DINOSAURS

Words and Music by Laurie Berkner

Strumming pattern (chorus):
Strumming pattern (verse):
Chorus
Bright March beat
Dm C Dm
We are the di - no - saurs, march - ing, march - ing. We are the
A Dm
di - no - saurs. Whad - da - ya think of that? We are the di - no - saurs,
C Dm A Dm C
march - ing, march - ing. We are the di - no - saurs. We make the earth
To Coda
Dm C Dm Verse F C
flat. We make the earth flat. We stop and eat our food
F C F C Dm F C
when we're in the mood. We stop and eat our food on the ground. We stop and eat our food
F C F C Dm A Interlude N.C.
rit.
when we're in the mood. We stop and eat our food and then we march a - round.
(drums)
Dm
'Cause... We are the di - no - saurs,
C Dm A
march - ing, march - ing. We are the di - no - saurs. Whad - da - ya think of

Dm C
that? We are the di - no - saurs, march - ing, march - ing.
Dm A Dm C Dm C
We are the di - no - saurs. We make the earth flat. We make the earth
Dm Verse F C F C F C
flat. We stop and take a rest o - ver in our nest. We stop and take our rest at the
Dm F C F C F C rit.
end of the day. We stop and take a rest o - ver in our nest. We stop and take a rest and then you'll
Dm A Interlude N.C. D.C. al Coda
hear us say (drums) that...
CODA Dm A freely
flat. And then we roar! 'Cause
Dm C D
we are the di - no - saurs. (roar)

WHEN I WOKE UP TODAY

Words and Music by Laurie Berkner

Strumming pattern:
Brightly
Guitar: (Capo I)
Piano:
When I woke up to - day, I shout - ed out, "Hoo - ray!" 'Cause
I knew I'd see you and we could sing to - geth - er.
La la la la la. La la la la la.
La la la la la la la la la. When
I woke up to - day, I shout - ed out, "Hoo - ray!" 'Cause
I knew I'd see you and we could shake to - geth - er.
tip - toe to - geth - er.
La la la la la. La la la la la.
La la la la la la la la la. When

2
B C F♯ G B C E F
When I woke up to - day, I shout - ed out, "Hoo - ray!"
F♯ G E F F♯ G E F
'Cause I knew I'd see you and we could jump and twist to - geth - er.
dance to - geth - er.
F♯ G B C F♯ G B C E F F♯ G
La la la la la. La la la la la.
E F F♯ G B C
La la la la la la la la la.
1
When
2
When
F♯ G B C E F F♯ G
I woke up to - day, I shout - ed out, "Hoo - ray!" 'Cause
E F F♯ G E F F♯ G
I knew I'd see you and there's no bet - ter thing to do than
E F F♯ G B C
sing a song and hear you sing it, too. La la la la.

ROCKETSHIP RUN

Words and Music by Laurie Berkner

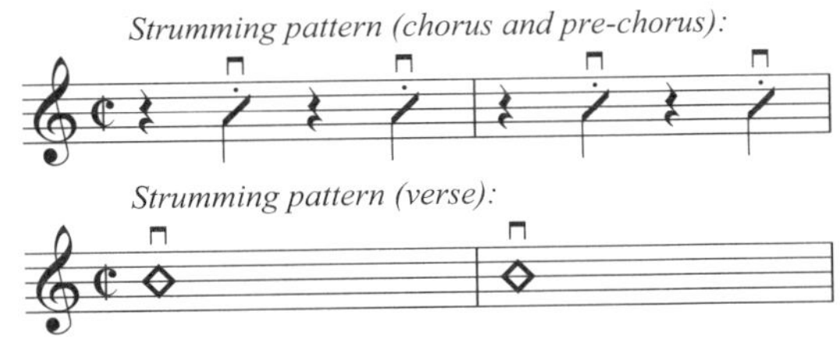
Strumming pattern (chorus and pre-chorus):
Strumming pattern (verse):

Chorus
Moderately, in 2
Am C G Am
Five, four, three, two, one, blast off! An-oth-er rock-et-ship run. Five, four, three, two, one,
To Coda
Verse
C G Am C G F
blast off! An-oth-er rock-et-ship run. 1. Take me to the sun.
2., 3. (See additional lyrics)
Pre-Chorus
C G F C G Am
Take me to the sun. When I get there, I'll go spin-ning
F C G F C
through the air, spin - ning 'round the sun.
G Am 1, 2 F 3 F D.C. al Coda
CODA
Verse
C G
Take me to the earth.
F C G F C
Leave me on the ground. When I
G Am Fmaj7
rit.
get there, I'll be home.
Chorus
Am F
a tempo
Ten, nine, eight,
G Am C G Am
sev - en, six, five, four, three, two, one, blast off! An - oth - er rock - et - ship run.

Additional Lyrics

2. Take me to the moon.
Take me to the moon.
When I get there, I'll go dancing through the air,
Dancing on the moon.

3. Take me to the stars.
Take me to the stars.
When I get there, I'll go jumping through the air,
Jumping from star to star.